Get Up And Lead!

Dynamic Downloads
For Leadership

By Apostle Dr. Cathy Coppola

© Copyright 2020 Cathy Coppola International Ministries

All rights reserved. No part of this publication may be reproduced, stored in a retrieval system, or transmitted in any form or by any means—electronic, mechanical, photocopy, recording, or any other—except for brief quotations in printed reviews, without the express written permission from the author. Reach her at:

Cathy Coppola International Ministries
P.O. Box 2923
Mission Viejo, CA 92691
www.cathycoppola.org
cathycoppola@gmail.com

Scripture marked (NKJV) is taken from the New King James Version®. Copyright © 1982 by Thomas Nelson. Used by permission. All rights reserved.

Scripture marked (NIV) is taken from THE HOLY BIBLE, NEW INTERNATIONAL VERSION®, NIV® Copyright © 1973, 1978, 1984, 2011 by Biblica, Inc.® Used by permission. All rights reserved worldwide.

Scripture marked (NASB) is taken from the NEW AMERICAN STANDARD BIBLE®, Copyright © 1960,1962,1963,1968,1971,1972,1973,1975,1977,1995 by The Lockman Foundation. Used by permission.

Scripture quotations marked (ESV) are from The ESV® Bible (The Holy Bible, English Standard Version®), copyright © 2001 by Crossway, a publishing ministry of Good News Publishers. Used by permission. All rights reserved.

Scripture quotations marked (AMP) are taken from the Amplified® Bible (AMP). Copyright © 2015 by The Lockman Foundation Used by permission. www.Lockman.org Scripture marked (BSB) is taken from The Holy Bible, Berean Study Bible, BSB Copyright ©2016, 2018 by Bible Hub Used by Permission. All Rights Reserved Worldwide.

Scripture quotations marked (NLT) are taken from the Holy Bible, New Living Translation, copyright © 1996, 2004, 2015 by Tyndale House Foundation. Used by permission of Tyndale House Publishers, Inc., Carol Stream, Illinois 60188. All rights reserved.

Scripture marked (KJV) is taken from the King James Version of the Holy Bible, which is in the public domain.

ISBN: 9798578973116

Table of Contents

Dedication	11
Introduction	13
1. Become Radically In Love With Jesus And Your God-Given Destiny Will Naturally Unfold.	15
2. Radical Lovers Are Ruined For The Ordinary.	17
3. My Only Regret Is That I Have But One Life On Earth To Give Him, But Grateful That I Can Live Forever In Eternity Thanking Him For All He Has Done.	19
4. If You Are Not Walking In Peace, You Are Not Walking In Jesus.	21
5. Let His Presence Consume You. Then Live From That Place.	23
6. Be So Filled With The Holy Spirit That Your Sight Is His Sight.	25
7. You Cannot Own What You Do Not See. See It Within First. Your Sight Will Determine Your Future.	27
8. You Are Crowned By The Creator. Multiply Yourself By Leading With Your Crown On. Royalty Multiplies Royalty.	29
9. Sons of God Serve Because It's A Privilege, Not A Duty. Serve As One With Full Rights And Your Servant Leadership Will Draw In Many.	31

10. Be An Influencer, Not A Controller. Rule Your Own Life And Be A Person Of Integrity. Others Will Desire What You Have And Glean From You. 35

11. You Always Have The Right To Choose; Even Your Silence Is A Choice. Choose Well. ... 37

12. Your Response Determines Your Outcome. ... 39

13. You Can't Control Other People's Lives, But You Can Rule Your Own. 41

14. Good Leaders Own Up To Their Faults And Apologize. 43

15. Good Leaders Refuel And Re-fire; They Don't Burn Out. 45

16. You Will Rise Or Fall At The Level Of Your Decision. Every Decision Determines Your Future. ... 47

17. It's Not About Popularity; It's About Inheritance. Your New Birth Provided Your Inheritance. Your Birthright Will Draw People. It's Your Heavenly Mark. 49

18. You Must Be A Leader Within Before You Can Lead Others. Lead Your Own Life Well And Others Will Follow. 51

19. You Cannot Lead Where You Have Not Gone. Your Current Trial Is Your Future Opportunity For Greater Influence. 53

20. Your Territory Is Your Domain. Exercise Your Right, Power, And Authority Over The Territory God Has Given You. 55

21. Live Life With Strength Under Control. A Horse Must Be Broken Before Its Strength Is Reliable. Let Your Brokenness Lead You To Strength Under God's Control.   57

22. A Disciplined Life Is A Successful Life, One Full Of Inheritance.   59

23. Scripture Is Like A Key. Use It To Unlock Doors. A Good Leader Knows Which Key To Use In Each Lock.   61

24. What You Value Reveals Who You Are. Your Convictions Are Your Values, And They Determine Your Character.   63

25. A Godly Leader Manifests The Character Of Christ, Even In Difficult Circumstances Because They Are Led By Their Convictions.   65

26. A Leader Will Have Followers. Be Self-Governed And Others Will Be Drawn To You.   67

27. Keep Your Life Centered On Christ, And Others Will Be Attracted To The Favor On Your Life.   69

28. Leadership Will Cost You. Only That Which Is Costly Is Ascribed Value. Don't Offer What Didn't Cost You Anything.   71

29. Good Leaders Lead Not Only By The Words Of Their Mouths But By The Actions Of Their Lives. Leaders Don't Let Their Words Contradict Their Actions. No One Wants To Follow A Hypocrite.   73

30. Leaders Love Even When It Is Difficult And Help Restore A Repentant Heart. 75

31. Godly Leaders Empower Others Without Fear Of Becoming Secondary. 77

32. Godly Leaders Encourage, Correct, And Affirm, In That Order, On Purpose. 79

33. Godly Leaders Lead So Others Know How To Follow. Lead With Kindness, Confidence, And Skill. 81

34. Leaders Teach What They Know But Reproduce Who They Are. After A Given Time, Those Under Your Influence Will Share Common Values And Principles. 83

35. Leaders Find Potential Key Leaders And Pour Their Lives Into Them. 85

36. Set Captives Free And Ignite Them With God's Love. 87

37. If God Has Entrusted You With A Leadership Position, Don't Disqualify What He Has Qualified. 89

38. A Good Leader Is A Good Delegator, One Who Leads By Example, By Telling You And By Showing You. 91

39. A Godly Leader Makes Hard Decisions For The Good Of All, Even When It's Costly. 93

40. A Godly Leader Trusts God Completely! Their Lives Exemplify His Peace. 95

41. A Good Leader Recognizes Time-Stealers As Gum On A Shoe. Quickly Change Shoes. 97

42. A Godly Leader Is Easily Recognized; Others Seek Out Your Counsel. 99
43. A Good Leader Sees The Potential In Others And Is Willing To Invest The Time To Develop Them. 101
44. Always Find One Thing You Learned From Your Challenge. Live And Grow Daily. 103
45. Challenges Are Opportunities To Grow. 105
46. Adversity Is An Opportunity, Not A Limitation. 107
47. Great Leaders Don't Despise Small Beginnings. 109
48. Great Leaders Are Faithful Where They Are Planted. 111
49. Great Leaders Exercise And Expand Their Gifts. 113
50. Great Leaders Overcome Adversity. 115
51. Great Leaders Always Remember Where They Came From And Remain Humble. 117
52. Good Leaders Know What to Stress and What to Overlook 119

Meet the Author 121

Dedication

I dedicate this book to future leaders who know their potential is higher than is evidenced in their lives today. It is time to arise and step in to who you were called to be. Lead with Christ-like character.

Introduction

The possibilities are endless! What does the Lord have for your future? Often times we limit Him and wonder why we don't feel fulfilled. I challenge you to read through this powerful book and allow the Lord to open your heart to all He has called you to be.

The road ahead is full of opportunities that will challenge you, but they have the potential to bring you into the fullest of your calling. Growth is possible but requires attention. Regardless of what you have been through, your future can be enriched and life-changing for others.

You are called to influence others and bring out the treasure in them as well. But how can you do this if you have not allowed Him to bring forth His strength in you?

Today marks a new day for you. Set aside a few moments a week to read that week's chapter. As you go through your week, allow the Lord to impress upon your heart the value of it and walk it out in your daily life.

These principles are a direct download from the

Heavenly Father. I know they will empower you to move forward in your life as you become a great leader. Lead with the love and power of our Almighty God and watch what He will do through you!

1. Become Radically In Love With Jesus And Your God-Given Destiny Will Naturally Unfold.

Your God-given destiny has been deposited within you! Jeremiah 29:11 (NIV) says, "For I know the plans I have for you," declares the Lord, "plans to prosper you and not to harm you, plans to give you hope and a future." Your future is wrapped up in Christ! As you find yourself in Him, you find yourself doing what He has called you to do. Let His love fill you, empower you, and overtake you, and you will be transformed into your destiny.

Allow His love to lavish you. Sit before Him and allow Him to overwhelm you with His incredible love. Let Him fill you with His all-consuming presence!

Your God-given destiny will naturally unfold. It will be a natural byproduct of a life lived in love with the King of Kings and Lord of Lords! When your identity is in Christ, you can flow in the power of the Spirit with an assurance that nothing can separate you from the love of God. The clouds broke open over Jesus when He was baptized in the Jordan River because He was in perfect union with the Father. When you gain your identity from heaven's breath over your life, you walk as a marked-out one, marked by His blood. The heavens parted and the Holy Spirit descended upon Him like a dove. The power of the Spirit will break through any barrier to bring you freedom. He is your strength in any storm.

Father, radically transform us, fill us with Your overwhelming love, and lead us into Your divine purpose.

"He will baptize you with the Holy Spirit and fire."

—Luke 3:16 (NIV)

2. Radical Lovers Are Ruined For The Ordinary.

Love God with everything within you, and live an extraordinary life. You were not created to be ordinary. You are extraordinary in Christ. Jesus took the water at the wedding in Cana and turned it into wine. He saved the best for last. As you follow His Word, your life will resemble His glory and carry His fragrance. Ordinary living is not your lot in life. Living in love with the one who loves you is. Live life radically for Him, radically in love and radically ruined for the ordinary. Let the fire of His heart burn deep within yours. God's pleasure in your life will be real to you as you walk under an open heaven. The only voice that will move you is the voice from heaven. When we are baptized by the Word and the Spirit, our ability to hear the Lord is imparted to us.

When Moses set his eyes on the burning bush, it transformed him! Moses had to flee from Egypt because he tried to deliver God's people through his own strength. But that had consequences. He killed the Egyptian and had to flee for his life. He had to leave everything he knew and go to the backside of the desert in Midian. He was reduced from the Prince of Egypt to a lowly shepherd. But one day his whole life was transformed when he set his eyes on the burning bush that was on fire but not consumed. It changed his life forever! He was completely transformed, and he was called into his destiny.

After God trained him up, He sent him back to Egypt to deliver His people His way. Moses had an encounter at the burning bush that was the presence of God! His presence will purify, purge, and propel you to do His purpose for your life. The "I AM that I AM" will set you ablaze for Him.

The Holy Spirit will come upon you in power to be an on-fire disciple of Christ. A life filled with the Holy Spirit is a life empowered to live fully for God.

Father, take my life and mold me into Your heart's desire. Cause me to yearn for Your radical love and transform me by Your power.

"Oh, taste and see that the LORD is good; Blessed is the man who trusts in Him!"

—Psalm 34:8 (NKJV)

3. My Only Regret Is That I Have But One Life On Earth To Give Him, But Grateful That I Can Live Forever In Eternity Thanking Him For All He Has Done.

Is your life wasteful or priceless? What the world considers wasteful, the Lord says is priceless. In Matthew 26:7, a woman has an alabaster flask of very costly fragrant oil that she pours on Jesus' head. The oil was costly, the flask was broken, and the oil was poured out. Costly oil from the wells of salvation has been your portion not only to take in but to give back. What you went through was costly; it left you broken so you can be a poured-out one for Him. Pour out your fragrant oil unto the Lord. Live for Jesus and spend your life on Him. Pour your life out on Him and lead others to do the same. Be His fragrance that brings life! One laid-down life spent on His presence brings the pleasure and favor of God into your life! You don't really live until you live for Christ. He has made a way for the broken and the hurting to come and fellowship with the Maker of heaven and earth. His presence will unfold your true identity and purpose in life and bring you to a fulfilled life in Him.

Others will be blessed when you live life in love with Christ.

Father, make me an offering poured out to you, and let the fragrance of Your love be evident to all. Let your encompassing presence draw many into Your kingdom.

"For we are to God the pleasing aroma of Christ among those who are being saved and those who are perishing."

—2 Corinthians 2:15 (NIV)

4. If You Are Not Walking In Peace, You Are Not Walking In Jesus.

True peace is found only in Christ. When you realize you have lost your peace, realize you have exchanged His perfect gift for the enemy's lie. It is your privilege as a son or daughter of God to regain His perfect provision and walk in the fullness of it. Regain peace by refocusing on Jesus, who is your Prince of Peace. Don't live life exchanging God's best gifts for the devil's counterfeit. You were created to live in peace and make decisions from that peace. Leadership will cost you. Opposition is inevitable. You will pay for what you value, and what you value you will reproduce. Be in remembrance of past victories as you move forward in Christ's unshakable peace. All ministry involves spiritual warfare. Be prepared for battle and quick to aid those who are under spiritual attack. You will be called to the frontlines during certain seasons, and during those times there is no room to relax your grip. Some seasons require intense war, so stay aware of Satan's schemes. Live alert and stay close to the Lord.

"He said: 'Listen, King Jehoshaphat and all who live in Judah and Jerusalem! This is what the Lord *says to you: "Do not be afraid or discouraged because of this vast army. For the battle is not yours, but God's."'"*

—2 Chronicles 20:15 (NIV)

"Through His name we trample down those who rise up against us. Through You we will push down our enemies; Through Your name we will trample those who rise up against us."

—*Psalm 44:5 (NKJV)*

"What then shall we say to these things? If God is for us, who can be against us?"

—*Romans 8:31 (NKJV)*

Father, our eyes shall be fixed on Jesus, the Prince of Peace. Lead us by Your perfect peace. We refocus the eyes of our spirit man on You. Help us focus on Your ability to keep us during any storm and trust that You will bring beauty out of it all. We choose to remain yielded to the Holy Spirit.

"For to us a child is born, to us a son is given, and the government will be on his shoulders. And he will be called Wonderful Counselor, Mighty God, Everlasting Father, Prince of Peace."

—*Isaiah 9:6 (NIV)*

5. Let His Presence Consume You. Then Live From That Place.

He is a consuming fire! When all you have is all He is, you become consumed and He becomes your dwelling place. Let Him purge you of all that will not bring Him pleasure and allow Him to transform you into a vessel of honor who knows who the divine creator is. When you are consumed in Him, then He is all that remains.

Dwell with Him in the fire of His presence and live on fire for Him! The challenges you face are really just opportunities for your growth! David had the anointing before the crown was visible even if he did not feel anointed. In 1 Samuel 16:1, the Lord provided Himself a king among Jesse's sons. Always remember that God sees your hiddenness. He sees you right where you are!

In 1 Samuel 16:12, the Lord instructed the prophet Samuel to anoint David to be the next king over Israel!

In 1 Samuel 16:13, Samuel took the horn of oil and anointed David in the midst of his brothers, and the Spirit of the Lord came upon David from that day forward.

The anointing on David's life would also create great challenges for him, which determined the longevity of his crown. A distressing spirit troubled Saul but tried to kill David because in the absence of the Spirit of God, men are vulnerable to evil spirits. Saul was not submitted to God; therefore, he was a pawn in the devil's hand.

The enemy saw David's potential and tried to sabotage it before it even began.

But the enemy is powerless when God's people walk in humble submission to the Lord.

1 Peter 5:8 says the enemy walks around like a roaring lion seeking whom it can devour, but the eyes of the Lord are upon the righteous and His ear is attentive to their cry. God sees all. Psalm 34:15, Proverbs 15:3

Let the presence of the Lord fill you to overflowing and then live from that place, trusting that the God who sees you will promote you in due time.

Father, consume me! All I want is all You are! Give me Your heart in every matter and lead me by Your sweet Holy Spirit.

"The fire must be kept burning on the altar continually; it must not go out."

—Leviticus 6:13 (NIV)

6. Be So Filled With The Holy Spirit That Your Sight Is His Sight.

The Holy Spirit will teach you all things and empower you to "see" as He sees. When your sight is His sight, watch how He unfolds your life and makes you His voice in this generation. Mary Magdalene saw the resurrected Christ and went to tell others. Though she saw Him, they did not believe her. Mark 16:9-11 Be so filled with the Holy Spirit that even when others don't believe what the Lord has done in your life, you will run forward and not let their doubt fill you with unbelief.

The Lord called David to be king over Israel when David was still in the field, keeping the sheep. He was dismissed by his father but called forward by God's prophet, Samuel, who anointed him with the horn of oil.

God saw significance in what others deemed insignificant. He chooses the foolish things of the world to shame the wise. The weak to shame the strong. 1 Corinthians 1:27 God knows you by name. Your calling will produce challenges, which should be viewed as opportunities for further growth. Like David, you are not an afterthought to God, for before He formed you, He knew you!

Father, fill me with the power of the Holy Spirit daily and give me Your eyes to see. Let me see Jesus in every person. Give me Your heart for this generation and make me Your mouthpiece, bringing Your truth to every nation.

"Then Jesus spoke to them again, saying, 'I am the light of the world. He who follows Me shall not walk in darkness, but have the light of life.'"

—John 8:12 (NKJV)

7. You Cannot Own What You Do Not See. See It Within First. Your Sight Will Determine Your Future.

Step into your future by seeing what God has for you. Ask Him for vision and the plan to walk it out. Then write it down and make it plain. It's time to implement it now! See the author in you, even though you have not written yet, and don't be discouraged when others don't have sight for it! See the preacher, the worship leader, or the business owner God has put in you. Keep the words God shares with you visible on a daily basis. Put the vision in a place where you will be reminded of it each and every day, especially on days where nothing in your life seems to be in alignment. Satan will use circumstances and people to cause you to doubt what God has said about your future. Silence his lies with the Word of God and your praise to the King of Kings.

See that you were called to be a forerunner to break the family's generational curse, the first to be saved, the first to run after Him, and don't let the ones who are spiritually blind cause you to lose sight. Keep your eyes on Jesus, the author and finisher of your faith!

Father, I cannot own what I don't see. Show me Your plan for my life. Give me a vision of what You have for me, and I will take the steps necessary to implement it.

"Where there is no vision, the people perish."

—Proverbs 29:18 (KJV)

*"Then the L*ORD *answered me and said: 'Write the vision And make it plain on tablets, That he may run who reads it.'"*

—Habakkuk 2:2 (NKJV)

8. You Are Crowned By The Creator. Multiply Yourself By Leading With Your Crown On. Royalty Multiplies Royalty.

When you said "Yes" to Jesus Christ, He became your Savior. You are now one with Him in Spirit; therefore, your identity is His identity. See yourself crowned by the creator, and multiply yourself by leading others to Him. You are His masterpiece. You can give others the treasure He has put in you.

Has He taught you of His great love? Go and share the Good News.

Has He taught you the value of forgiveness? Go out and share this with others.

Has He taught you how to completely trust in Him? The world is waiting for authentic believers who talk the talk and walk the walk. Go out and be a blessing to someone else.

Your personal testimony is attractive to other people. Nothing touches the heart more than someone who has experienced the same pain, addiction, or loss. God will provide the opportunities if you will share the Good News of freedom in Christ.

Father, You have crowned me with a royal diadem and clothed me with garments of praise and a robe of righteousness. Because of Jesus I can live in an authentic relationship with You and therefore bring others to Christ by the power of the Holy Spirit.

"But whoever is united with the Lord is one with Him in spirit."

—*1 Corinthians 6:17 (NIV)*

"To console those who mourn in Zion, To give them beauty for ashes, The oil of joy for mourning, The garment of praise for the spirit of heaviness...."

—*Isaiah 61:3 (NKJV)*

9. Sons of God Serve Because It's A Privilege, Not A Duty. Serve As One With Full Rights And Your Servant Leadership Will Draw In Many.

When circumstances tried to put Joseph into captivity as a slave in Egypt, the Lord still raised him up! A slave in Egypt, yet he found favor with both God and man.

The Lord blessed the Egyptian's house for Joseph's sake, and the blessing of the Lord was on ALL that he had in the house and in the field. Genesis 39:5

Nothing will change the fact that as the Lord was with Him, the Lord is also with you and will increase and prosper you in due time.

Joseph was falsely accused and placed in the King's prison, but the Lord was with him in the prison and gave him favor and promotion.

In prison he served by using the gift he had. He interpreted dreams. Because Joseph used the gift God gave him, the Lord made a way to raise him up and out of his unjust captivity.

After a thirteen-year affliction, Joseph's gift and wisdom brought him before great men and opened the door to his destiny.

Pharaoh placed him in charge over his house and over all the land of Egypt! Genesis 41:41 The Lord gave him power and authority in the very same plan of captivity the enemy devised for him.

The attacks against you are only going to prove that you will arise and overcome and all opposition against you for what the enemy meant for evil, the Lord will work it for good.

Be sure to use the gifts He gave you during that time. Don't wait to operate in the gifts of God. This is your training time. This is your preparation time. You are training for reigning.

"A man's gift makes room for him And brings him before great men."

—*Proverbs 18:16 (NKJV)*

"Do you see a man who excels in his work? He will stand before kings; He will not stand before unknown men."

—*Proverbs 22:29 (NKJV)*

Jesus was the greatest leader of all time. He said in His Word whoever wants to become great among you must be your servant.

—*Matthew 20:26*

A great leader is a great servant, a life that Jesus modeled for us. "I am among you as the One who serves." Luke 22:27 (NKJV) In serving, you see the heart of the Father and can lead like Jesus led. In serving, you experience the heart of the Father more and more.

Father, Jesus said in Mark 9:35 that if anyone wants to be first, he must be the last of all and the servant of all. In serving one another, we serve You, Father, for Matthew 25:40 says that whatever we did for one of the least of these brothers of Mine, you did for Me. Serving You is a privilege and one that should not be taken lightly. Let my servant leadership draw in many to the kingdom.

"And if anyone gives even a cup of cold water to one of these little ones who is my disciple, truly I tell you, that person will certainly not lose their reward."

—Matthew 10:42 (NIV)

10. Be An Influencer, Not A Controller. Rule Your Own Life And Be A Person Of Integrity. Others Will Desire What You Have And Glean From You.

Believers in Christ are the salt of the earth and the light of the world. Matthew 5:13-14 It is an honor to add value to others' lives. You are the salt and light that will make the difference in them. Influence them for Christ with godly integrity, and others will naturally desire what you carry. Give them Jesus! You may feel foolish, but God chose the foolish to put to shame the wise. You may feel weak, but God chose the weak to put to shame the strong. It's not about where you come from that matters the most but where you are going that matters.

Don't let your past define your future. The blood of Christ has marked you for royalty, not failure! Ruth did not allow her reputation as a Moabite woman to forfeit her future. If God could choose a Gentile woman whose national background was corrupt with sexual carnality and put her in the lineage of Jesus, what could He do with your life?

You may not know how much influence you have on other people's lives. As you face difficulty, obstacles, and slanderous talk, your reaction matters. As a leader, you can choose to rise above. When you choose not to react as the world expects, people will take notice. They will see something different about you. Walk in peace when there is conflict, strength when there is adversity, and integrity in the face of lies. The God who sees all will bring you forth as one He can entrust with the lives of many more people.

Father, You have deposited Your great love in me, and I choose to be a vessel of Your great outpouring in the lives of others. As I govern my life, let others be influenced to live for You, for You have made me both salt and light in this world.

"You are the salt of the earth. But if the salt loses its saltiness, how can it be made salty again? It is no longer good for anything, except to be thrown out and trampled underfoot.

You are the light of the world. A town built on a hill cannot be hidden. Neither do people light a lamp and put it under a bowl. Instead they put it on its stand, and it gives light to everyone in the house. In the same way, let your light shine before others, that they may see your good deeds and glorify your Father in heaven."

—Matthew 5:13-16 (NIV)

11. You Always Have The Right To Choose; Even Your Silence Is A Choice. Choose Well.

Today, the Lord has assigned you someone to minister to. Will you embrace the opportunities that await you and speak life to those around you? Every day you have choices. Even when you choose not to speak up, you have made a choice. Learn to use your words and your silence to bring about the truth of God's Word. Let God lead you as He ministers through you. Don't get ahead of God or forget your place.

Never remain silent when God is asking you to speak.

Never speak up when He has asked you to remain silent.

Ruth, a Moabitess, chose to remain connected to Naomi, an Israelite woman, who brought her out of the land of Moab and into the land of Bethlehem, the House of Bread. Her right choice and alignment set her up for being God's choice in her marriage to Boaz, her kinsmen redeemer. Your choices can either align or misalign you.

Elimelech's bad decision put Naomi and her kids in a predicament. Wisdom is given to the one who asks God. Naomi later made the right decision to redeem her family. Proverbs 1:33 Whoever listens to Me will dwell in safety and will be secure without fear of evil.

Father, I choose to be Your voice in this generation and take back what the enemy has stolen. I choose life abundantly. My words carry weight as I mix my faith with Your promises. Let my words bring healing and comfort to those You have entrusted me with.

> *"Learn to do good; Seek justice, Rebuke the oppressor; Defend the fatherless, Plead for the widow."*
>
> *—Isaiah 1:17 (NKJV)*

> *"Death and life are in the power of the tongue, And those who love it will eat its fruit."*
>
> *—Proverbs 18:21 (NKJV)*

12. Your Response Determines Your Outcome.

The response of the heart is the inner motive that will determine your outcome. What you speak and why you speak it is backed by what you believe and will result in what you receive. Every choice we make will determine our outcome. Remember to choose life so that you and your descendants shall live. What you have today is what you have partnered with Christ to give you. Don't let your tongue be used for the enemy's plans. Guard your heart by putting a guard over your mouth. His significance makes us significant. You were foreknown and predestined to be conformed to His image. Romans 8:29-30 (NKJV) says, "For whom He foreknew, He also predestined to be conformed to the image of His Son, that He might be the firstborn among many brethren. Moreover whom He predestined, these He also called; whom He called, these He also justified; and whom He justified, these He also glorified."

Moses had a lot of excuses, a lot of insecurities. While hidden in God, God dealt with his insecurities. Lord, not me, I stutter. I mix up words. I get tongue tied. Surely you can find someone else. Exodus 4:10-13 All of us can feel inadequate whenever God asks us to do something because His divine plan is always bigger than anything we can dream or desire. Don't let your insecurities become your excuse. Let them become your place of dependence on God.

A miscarriage occurs when a woman's body rejects the fetus she is carrying. We can spiritually miscarry something by rejecting it intentionally or unintentionally. The vision is for an appointed time, and it must be carried to full term. Some reject the calling because of the level of warfare it brings. The anointing on your life will bring certain levels of persecution. Persecution may be validation that your calling is from God. Judas, one of the twelve disciples, didn't step into his calling because the level of warfare outweighed his character. If you don't carry out the prophetic release over your life, someone else will.

Mary said in Luke 1:38, "Let it be to me…." (NKJV)

Father, it is my response that determines my outcome in life. I choose to place myself under the authority of Your Word to lead and guide my reply. I choose to let Your Word direct my speech, and I will see Your faithfulness come to pass.

"Set a guard, O LORD, over my mouth; Keep watch over the door of my lips."

—Psalm 141:3 (NKJV)

"I call heaven and earth as witnesses today against you, that I have set before you life and death, blessing and cursing; therefore choose life, that both you and your descendants may live."

—Deuteronomy 30:19 (NKJV)

13. You Can't Control Other People's Lives, But You Can Rule Your Own.

The process of eliminating the irritant is how the oyster forms a pearl. Stop trying to eliminate the irritant prematurely. Learn that a life yielded to the Lord during trials and adversities forms your outward and inward glow. It's costly, yet it's worth it all. The glow produced in your life will be a byproduct of strength under fire.

When you feel afflicted and it seems to go on and on, go to the Lord for advice. Seek the Lord above all things and find wisdom to endure.

Learn to be self-controlled in the trials of life, for self-control is one of the fruits of the Spirit found in Galatians 5:22-23. When you walk in self-control, you will govern your own life.

Proverbs 25:28 says whoever has no rule over his own spirit, no self-control, is like a city broken down without walls. If your life is like a city broken down without walls, you are exposed and vulnerable to all forms of attack by the enemy. Learn to walk in self-control. Rule, self-govern, and own your own life. Don't be so quick to eliminate the irritant. It is the process that produces great depth and strength in your life. Do not let purpose fall to the ground. Let it be passed to the next generation. You were never meant to magnify the warfare or shrink back because of it. You are anointed to break the yoke and strip the enemy of power.

Father, I cannot control what others do or say, but I certainly can control my response and my actions. I choose to govern my own life regardless of and in spite of what I am exposed to. By the wisdom of God, I can and will stay focused and on track and become one You can entrust with the lives of many people.

"But the fruit of the Spirit is love, joy, peace, forbearance, kindness, goodness, faithfulness, gentleness and self-control. Against such things there is no law."

—Galatians 5:22-23 (NIV)

14. Good Leaders Own Up To Their Faults And Apologize.

Walking in true humility is the only real way to live an overcoming life. When you recognize your faults and apologize, this speaks louder than any good deed done. Humility and repentance is the language of true Christianity. Model the behavior you want to see, and you will find your submission to Christ leading many to live with godly purpose and authenticity!

Mistakes, errors, and poor decisions are part of everyday life. A true godly leader will not point fingers but own up to their faults. People respond to a leader who holds themselves accountable to someone in their life. Truth and vulnerability are not found in all leaders but in those who are a reflection of Jesus to the world.

Father, You said if we confess our sins, You would be faithful and just to forgive us our sins and to cleanse us from all unrighteousness. 1 John 1:9 We confess our faults to You and commit to make it right with the person we have sinned against. Father, let our submission to You be pleasing in Your sight. Teach us to lead by example to everyone around us. Our desire is to model the love of God to all we meet.

"Likewise you younger people, submit yourselves to your elders. Yes, all of you be submissive to one another, and be clothed with humility, for 'God resists the proud, But gives grace to the humble.' Therefore humble yourselves under the mighty hand of God, that He may exalt you in due time."

—1 Peter 5:5-6 (NKJV)

15. Good Leaders Refuel And Re-fire; They Don't Burn Out.

The enemy wants to exhaust you and cause you to burn out, but as we stay connected to the vine, we will never burn out! Stay in fellowship with the Creator and He will constantly feed you all you need. The vine is always producing life, and the branches receive their life source from it.

Nehemiah was a man of prayer. He never quit doing the will of God even though he had much opposition trying to get him to do so. In fifty-two days, he erected the walls of Jerusalem that were once broken down and the gates that had been burned by fire. As Nehemiah exemplified great strength under fire, we too must stay on task, doing the will of God regardless of the incredible opposition that comes against us, knowing that when we do the will of God, every detractor and accuser will try to distract us, but God's power is available to carry us through if we don't quit.

Lead others but never forget to be led yourself by the King of Kings. Daily He will anoint you with fresh oil as you make time to commune with Him. Psalm 90:10

Father, daily I come to You to drink from Your presence. I take in Your provision, Your creative power, Your ability to forgive, Your grace to lead like Jesus, Your wisdom and knowledge and anointing to walk in the Holy Spirit's power to all I meet today.

"Come to me, all you who are weary and burdened, and I will give you rest."

—Matthew 11:28 (NIV)

*"But those who wait on the L*ORD *Shall renew their strength; They shall mount up with wings like eagles, They shall run and not be weary, They shall walk and not faint."*

—Isaiah 40:31 (NKJV)

16. You Will Rise Or Fall At The Level Of Your Decision. Every Decision Determines Your Future.

Don't shortchange yourself. Elijah did not shorten his time at the brook Cherith. What he did not know was while he was hidden away at the brook, Jezebel had prophets of God killed. Had Elijah not been hidden, his life would have been cut short. Maybe your season of hiddenness is God's protection over your life, but you thought it was a punishment.

Make decisions based on a yielded life in the Holy Spirit. Every decision will amount to an outcome.

Guard your mouth and preserve your life. Allow the Spirit of Truth to lead your decisions and rise up and take the place God has marked out for you. Never allow a quick, thoughtless, prayerless decision to remain in place.

Every decision results in an outcome that can alter your assignment. Make sure you have asked the Lord for His eyes to see what you cannot see before you move forward.

Father, I choose to follow Your perfect will in my life. Give me wisdom and discernment as I move through this day, and quicken me by Your Holy Spirit to always walk with the mind of Christ.

"...Choose for yourselves this day whom you will serve...."

—Joshua 24:15 (NKJV)

"A man shall eat well by the fruit of his mouth, But the soul of the unfaithful feeds on violence."

—Proverbs 13:2 (NKJV)

17. It's Not About Popularity; It's About Inheritance. Your New Birth Provided Your Inheritance. Your Birthright Will Draw People. It's Your Heavenly Mark.

The Lord is not looking at the outward but the inward. He looks at the heart. Your new birth in Christ provided for you more than you may realize. More than any person could offer. More than any achievement could attain. More than any self-efforts could produce. Your inheritance in Christ marked you with the living Savior seeded deep within you. Holy living is more important than walking in a form of godliness but denying true power. You have become marked with heaven's riches. Go out and share the Good News of the gospel.

Father, in You I have received a living hope, an inheritance that will never perish, never spoil, and never dissolve. I am known and valued in heaven. Earth is temporary but eternity with You will last forever. I choose to live from a place of being marked out for Christ, enjoying heaven's riches even before I arrive there, for You dwell within me.

"Praise be to the God and Father of our Lord Jesus Christ! In his great mercy he has given us new birth into a living hope through the resurrection of Jesus Christ from the dead, and into an inheritance that can never perish, spoil or fade. This inheritance is kept in heaven for you."

—1 Peter 1:3-4 (NIV)

18. You Must Be A Leader Within Before You Can Lead Others. Lead Your Own Life Well And Others Will Follow.

Think before taking action; then step out in great boldness. Be committed to obedience to God's will. Learn to recognize demonic strength coming against you and be victorious over it. Conspiracy, confusion, slander, lies, mockery, and intimidation are all part of Satan's schemes. Distress should lead you to fast and pray. Every great man or woman of God will be put through the fire and tested. The weight of your circumstances may feel heavy, but it will not crush you. The enemy only resists those who are going somewhere. Like Nehemiah, be ready to serve others and lead them to rebuild and restore with the Word in your mouth and the sword in your hand.

Allow the Lord to make you a great leader first by being a great servant. Then in serving, God will use you to lead others well. Good leaders must always make sure their hearts are kept right by allowing the Holy Spirit to speak to them. What doesn't please the Father will grieve the Holy Spirit within you. Learn not to dismiss the nudging of the Spirit. Learn to rule your own spirit and be self-governed. Live by God's Word and He will mold you into a person He can trust with His children.

Father, teach me to self-govern my own life by living in obedience to Your Word. Train me to rule over my human spirit and keep my heart with all diligence. I don't want to lead anyone astray. Leading others is a great responsibility. In all I do, my desire is to please You. Teach me to self-govern and draw those You have assigned to me.

"Keep your heart with all diligence for out of it spring the issues of life."

—Proverbs 4:23 (NKJV)

"Whoever has no rule over his own spirit is like a city broken down, without walls."

—Proverbs 25:28 (NKJV)

19. You Cannot Lead Where You Have Not Gone. Your Current Trial Is Your Future Opportunity For Greater Influence.

Your current trial is your future opportunity for greater influence. Allow the lessons learned in this season to shape you. There is a leader within you that the Lord is getting ready to use for His glory. But you cannot lead others where you have not gone. The greater the pain, the greater the glory. But that glory is not for you; it belongs to the Lord. Glorify God with all He gives you. After the storm, the sun will shine. Shine for Christ and watch Him do exceedingly, abundantly above all you ask or think, according to the power that works in you. Ephesians 3:20 Remember, the presence of evil is not the void of God's power in your life, but the proof that God's power trumps wickedness for the one who remains faithful to Him.

Father, I thank You for seeing in me what I may not even see in myself. Use me for Your glory. In all I do, in all that comes against me, in every situation I choose to lay my life down so I can be a vessel that brings You glory and leaves a beautiful legacy behind.

"Now to Him who is able to do exceedingly abundantly above all that we ask or think, according to the power that works in us, to Him be glory in the church by Christ Jesus to all generations, forever and ever. Amen."

—Ephesians 3:20-21 (NKJV)

20. Your Territory Is Your Domain. Exercise Your Right, Power, And Authority Over The Territory God Has Given You.

What you allow, you empower. So, what are you empowering? Your territory is your domain. Exercise your right, power, and authority over the territory God has given you. Luke 10: 19 says every believer has been given authority to do something. What are you doing with the authority God has given you? Trample on every serpent and scorpion spirit the enemy sends against you. Your future depends on it. Trample on every spirit of unbelief, fear, and intimidation. Trample on every assignment meant to keep you voiceless, powerless, and ineffective. The enemy thought he had you on the run until he saw you were not running from him, but toward God!

Father, we stand on Luke 10:19 and exercise our God-given authority to trample on serpents and scorpions and over the power of the enemy, and nothing shall by any means hurt us. We take back our authority and render the enemy voiceless, powerless, and ineffective over our lives, in Jesus' name.

"And these signs will follow those who believe: In My name they will cast out demons; they will speak with new tongues; they will take up serpents; and if they drink anything deadly, it will by no means hurt them; they will lay hands on the sick, and they will recover."

—*Mark 16:17-18 (NKJV)*

21. Live Life With Strength Under Control. A Horse Must Be Broken Before Its Strength Is Reliable. Let Your Brokenness Lead You To Strength Under God's Control.

Strength is not strength unless it is under control. Strength under control will lead you to places an unruly spirit never will. Allow your strength to be in submission to the Lord, and let Him break you where you need it.

He will then use you in ways you never thought possible, but He will get all the glory. Allow your insecurities and your confidence to be under the submission of the Lord. Give Him your hopes and your disappointments and watch Him mold you into His glorious masterpiece, entrusting you with a greater sphere of people because your strength is now under His control.

Father, You give strength to the weary and increase the power of the weak. Work in me and mold me. I repent for any unruly place in my soul.

Father, I choose to walk in obedience to Your Word. Strip away all that is unruly, ungodly, and unbecoming from me. Lead me to live life with strength under Your control.

"Do not be like the horse or like the mule, Which have no understanding, Which must be harnessed with bit and bridle, Else they will not come near you."

—Psalm 32:9 (NKJV)

22. A Disciplined Life Is A Successful Life, One Full Of Inheritance.

When I think of the word *discipline*, I am reminded of consistency. We can live a disciplined life when we live a life consistent in prayer, consistent in reading the Word of God, consistent in giving, and so on.

Slow and steady wins the race. Sometimes people think they have to race to the finish line. But in reality, life is about being consistent and persevering through it all. In consistency you will live disciplined and receive your full inheritance. You will recognize God's treasure along the way and not lose out on His daily provision.

Reaching the end of your race without enjoying the daily benefits of living a disciplined life only results in winning a prize but failing to receive the joy that the prize offers.

Father, a disciplined life is a successful life. I stand on Your Word and declare I will not become weary in doing good, for Your Word is my strength, and You said I will reap a harvest if I do not give up. You said those You love You rebuke, and You discipline. Correction from the Lord leads to the peaceful fruit of righteousness to those who have been trained by it. Hebrews 12:11 Mold me and make me like You. In Jesus' name.

"No discipline seems pleasant at the time, but painful. Later on, however, it produces a harvest of righteousness and peace for those who have been trained by it."

—*Hebrews 12:11 (NIV)*

"Let us not become weary in doing good, for at the proper time we will reap a harvest if we do not give up."

—Galatians 6:9 (NIV)

23. Scripture Is Like A Key. Use It To Unlock Doors. A Good Leader Knows Which Key To Use In Each Lock.

The key of David symbolizes the key of authority in Isaiah 22:22. Revelation 3:7 tells us the door He opens no one can shut, and the door He shuts no one can open. There are doors you are to unlock, but the only way you will be able to unlock them is as you stand in oneship with the Word of God. Using His Word will unlock things for you that the enemy has kept from you. Use your keys of authority to bind what is unlawful and to loose what is lawful in your life. It is time to step out into more!

Father, we use the key of David You gave us, which is our authority to stand on Your Word and decree it.

We bind all demonic attacks and forbid them access into our lives. We loose heaven's provision and decree that every door you have opened for us shall remain open, and every door You see fit to close shall remain closed in Jesus' name. We unlock the blocked access to Your revelation in our lives. We decree, we thrive, and we cause others to thrive with every door we walk through in Jesus' name.

"I will give you the keys (authority) of the kingdom of heaven; and whatever you bind [forbid, declare to be improper and unlawful] on earth will have [already] been bound in heaven, and whatever you loose [permit, declare lawful] on earth will have [already] been loosed in heaven."

—Matthew 16:19 (AMP)

24. What You Value Reveals Who You Are. Your Convictions Are Your Values, And They Determine Your Character.

You are who God says you are. You are created in God's image, drawn by Him with an everlasting love, and redeemed with the precious blood of Jesus Christ. Value God's Word above culture, above tradition, and above feelings, for His Word will mark you out and give you a future and a hope. Choosing to have a godly character in every circumstance will set you apart from the crowd. That is what will define you. That is why people can trust you. They see Christ in you. Let them see Jesus in you daily as you make no provision for the flesh. Choose to live by the Spirit, producing the fruit of the Spirit.

Father, may my life exemplify Christ. May my character cause others to want to lay their lives down for Him. For nothing compares with a life lived in Christ. My old life has passed away. Now I live to declare His goodness in every area of my life.

"Therefore, if anyone is in Christ, he is a new creation; old things have passed away; behold, all things have become new."

—2 Corinthians 5:17 (NKJV)

"Rather, clothe yourselves with the Lord Jesus Christ, and do not think about how to gratify the desires of the flesh."

—Romans 13:14 (NIV)

25. A Godly Leader Manifests The Character Of Christ, Even In Difficult Circumstances Because They Are Led By Their Convictions.

What you tolerate you become! What are your convictions? Do they raise Jesus above yourself? Your firm beliefs and opinions are being used to mold others. But how are they molding them? A godly leader manifests God's heart, regardless of the pain endured, because they have been transformed into His likeness, and now they live for Him. Don't blame others. The very ones who should have known better were manipulated like pawns in the devil's hands. 1 Peter 5:8 When you were torn down, it came at a cost, but now the devil is paying, and he never saw it coming. Deuteronomy 28:7

Father, I have found the one my heart loves in You! My very being now thirsts for Your presence moment by moment. I live to glorify You. Father, let me be consistent in leading my own life with godly convictions, and convict me when I begin to stray.

"He who speaks from himself seeks his own glory; but He who seeks the glory of the One who sent Him is true, and no unrighteousness is in Him."

—John 7:18 (NKJV)

"I delight to do Your will, O my God; And Your Law is within my heart."

—Psalm 40:8 (NKJV)

26. A Leader Will Have Followers. Be Self-Governed And Others Will Be Drawn To You.

A good leader will make sure they are always building others up, not tearing others down.

They apply the same rules to themselves that they apply to others. Are you inwardly tearing yourself down? If so, this is self-destructive and will short-circuit what the Lord has for you. We must be able to self-govern our lives before we can be entrusted to offer help to someone else. This begins with the first commandment: "...'You shall love the LORD your God with all your heart, with all your soul, and with all your mind.' This is the first and great commandment. And the second is like it: 'You shall love your neighbor as yourself.'" Matthew 22:37-39 (NKJV)

When we can learn to love ourselves, we can love others. The gift of love is what will draw others to you, and then you can be entrusted to add value to their lives for the kingdom.

Father, in loving myself I can love others and influence them for Your kingdom. Teach me to love when I am afraid, love when I have been hurt, love when I have been discarded or rejected. Make me one whom others are drawn to, and give me the wisdom to lead like Jesus led.

"But seek first the kingdom of God and His righteousness, and all these things shall be added to you."

—Matthew 6:33 (NKJV)

27. Keep Your Life Centered On Christ, And Others Will Be Attracted To The Favor On Your Life.

The Bible says "Blessed are the pure in heart, for they will see God." Matthew 5:8 (NIV)

It also says He blesses the righteous and surrounds them with favor. Psalm 5:12 As we keep our life centered on Christ, we keep our hearts pure. Don't be caught off guard. Stay focused. Stay centered in His will by staying in His Word. His life in you will produce great results. His favor on your life will be evident to all.

His favor lasts a lifetime.

Father, Your favor will surround me, and your blessings will overflow in my life. Keep me as the apple of Your eye, and hide me under the shadow of Your wings, for in You I long to live all day long. Let others be led to You by the favor on my life.

"Surely, LORD, you bless the righteous; you surround them with your favor as with a shield."

—Psalm 5:12 (NIV)

"For his anger lasts only a moment, but his favor lasts a lifetime; weeping may stay for the night but rejoicing comes in the morning."

—Psalm 30:5 (NIV)

28. Leadership Will Cost You. Only That Which Is Costly Is Ascribed Value. Don't Offer What Didn't Cost You Anything.

Many want to offer value, but they don't want to pay the price associated with attaining that value.

Value gained is insight lived. Only what counts for eternity is valuable. Are you willing to lose what you love if it means you may gain eternal life? Some things are good, but good is the enemy of best. Good will rob you of God's best. His best is a life spent living for Him. Live life dead to self and selfish motives and alive to His leading. When we die, we gain. We gain eternity's perspective. The cost of dying will gain an eternal reward.

Father, I will not offer to You what did not cost me anything. Burnt offerings that cost me nothing gain nothing. But a life lived in secret obedience unto You, my King, is a life lived fully surrendered and yielded to You, no matter what comes against me. Let my life be a fragrant offering rising up to Your Throne.

"Very truly I tell you, unless a kernel of wheat falls to the ground and dies, it remains only a single seed. But if it dies, it produces many seeds. Anyone who loves their life will lose it, while anyone who hates their life in this world will keep it for eternal life."

—John 12:24-25 (NIV)

"But King David replied to Araunah, 'No, I insist on paying the full price. I will not take for the L<small>ORD</small> what is yours, or sacrifice a burnt offering that costs me nothing.'"

—*1 Chronicles 21:24 (NIV)*

29. Good Leaders Lead Not Only By The Words Of Their Mouths But By The Actions Of Their Lives. Leaders Don't Let Their Words Contradict Their Actions. No One Wants To Follow A Hypocrite.

When your words please the Lord and they match your heart's response, God can use you for greater things.

No one wants to follow a person who talks the talk but does not walk the walk. Be genuine in your day-to-day responses. If you allow the Holy Spirit to speak through you, you will find He places a guard on your mouth and tenderizes your heart so you become authentic and not a hypocrite.

Father, "Let the words of my mouth and the meditation of my heart be acceptable in Your sight, O LORD, my strength, and my redeemer." Psalm 19:14 (NKJV)

"A good man out of the good treasure of his heart brings forth good; and an evil man out of the evil treasure of his heart brings forth evil. For out of the abundance of the heart his mouth speaks."

—Luke 6:45 (NKJV)

"And Jabez called on the God of Israel saying, 'Oh, that You would bless me indeed, and enlarge my territory, that Your hand would be with me, and that You would keep me from evil, that I may not cause pain!' So God granted him what he requested."

—1 Chronicles 4:10 (NKJV)

30. Leaders Love Even When It Is Difficult And Help Restore A Repentant Heart.

If someone has repented, will you do good to them when it is in your power to do so? Will you do good to them when they were the cause of your pain? The Bible says in Proverbs 3:27 (NKJV), "Do not withhold good from those to whom it is due, When it is in the power of your hand to do so." Treat others the way you would want to be treated. Give the gift of mercy. For if you give mercy, you shall find mercy.

Lay down your life daily and help restore those around you.

Your Heavenly Father sees. Your Heavenly Father is the Great Rewarder.

Father, because of the forgiveness I have received from Christ, I can offer forgiveness and help restore the repentant heart that at one time caused me great pain. Mercy extended to others affords me favor in the sight of God and man.

"The sacrifices of God are a broken spirit, A broken and a contrite heart—These, O God, You will not despise."

—Psalm 51:17 (NKJV)

"Let not mercy and truth forsake you; Bind them around your neck, Write them on the tablet of your heart, And so find favor and high esteem in the sight of God and man."

—Proverbs 3:3-4 (NKJV)

"But without faith it is impossible to please Him, for he who comes to God must believe that He is, and that He is a rewarder of those who diligently seek Him."

—Hebrews 11:6 (NKJV)

31. Godly Leaders Empower Others Without Fear Of Becoming Secondary.

Godly leaders lead from a place of inner strength and security, knowing it was the Lord who promoted them in the first place, and it will be the Lord who will keep them where He wants them.

There is no fear when you walk in God's perfect love. Fear of losing your position reveals a lack of trusting the Lord, who placed you in that position in the first place.

Father, You know the end from the beginning. Promotion comes from God. As You have promoted me, give me sight to see whom I should invest time into. Use me to raise up those You have called and appointed.

"For promotion cometh neither from the east, nor from the west, nor from the south. But God is the judge: he putteth down one, and setteth up another."

—Psalm 75:6-7 (KJV)

*"But now, thus says the L*ORD*, who created you, O Jacob, And He who formed you, O Israel: 'Fear not, for I have redeemed you; I have called you by your name; You are Mine.'"*

—Isaiah 43:1 (NKJV)

32. Godly Leaders Encourage, Correct, And Affirm, In That Order, On Purpose.

The Bible says in Matthew 7:12 (NKJV), "…whatever you want men to do to you, do also to them…."

As a person who has influence over others, you want to treat others as you want to be treated.

Be one who encourages before correcting. Learn to affirm what is good before pointing out what needs to change. The order is important. The goal is to raise up godly leaders and influence them to be strong in the Lord to those they have been called to minister to. Learn to speak the language of affirmation, not flattery. Speak truth, encourage, correct, and affirm, in that order, on purpose.

Father, You loved us even when we were lost in our sin. You choose to love and make a way for us to come to the saving knowledge of Jesus Christ. We follow Your example in drawing people. Love always makes a way for influence! Cause us to really love others and lead from a place of caring. Teach us to see what is good in others before pointing out what needs to change. Teach us to be godly leaders who are still learning ourselves.

"All Scripture is God-breathed and is useful for teaching, rebuking, correcting and training in righteousness, so that the servant of God may be thoroughly equipped for every good work."

—2 Timothy 3:16-17 (NIV)

"Hypocrite! First remove the plank from your own eye, and then you will see clearly to remove the speck from your brother's eye."

—Matthew 7:5 (NKJV)

"Instead, speaking the truth in love, we will grow to become in every respect the mature body of him who is the head, that is, Christ."

—Ephesians 4:15 (NIV)

33. Godly Leaders Lead So Others Know How To Follow. Lead With Kindness, Confidence, And Skill.

The closer you are to Jesus, the more you become aware of your own faults.

Paul wrote in 1 Timothy 1:15 that he is the worst of all sinners. And in Galatians 6:14 he said to never boast except in the cross.

When God calls you to a position of having influence over others, how you lead is very important.

When Joseph was placed in a position of power, he did not use his power to dominate or control his brothers. Genesis 50:19-21

Instead he led with kindness, confidence and skill. Never forget where you've come from and don't ever let the power you have frighten others. Lead like Jesus led.

Father, I desire to be a person after Your heart. Let me always lead with kindness, confidence and skill.

Draw those to me who need to be mentored and led by what You have given me.

"But Joseph said to them, "Don't be afraid. Am I in the place of God? You intended to harm me, but God intended it for good to accomplish what is now being done, the saving of many lives.

So then, don't be afraid. I will provide for you and your children." And he reassured them and spoke kindly to them."

—Genesis 50:19-21 (NIV)

34. Leaders Teach What They Know But Reproduce Who They Are. After A Given Time, Those Under Your Influence Will Share Common Values And Principles.

People will see and follow your values and your belief system. Your words may catch their attention, but who you are will draw them. Be a person who is genuine and authentic. Lead from truth. Be confident that what the Lord has taught you thus far will benefit those you minister to. Release the Word, but make sure you are living the Word and not just speaking it. Give it time and you will see others enriched because you cared enough to pour out to them what the Lord poured out to you.

Father, all I have is from You. I give You all the glory for it. Continue to use me for Your glory in the lives of others.

"You are the salt of the earth; but if the salt has become tasteless, how can it be made salty again? It is no longer good for anything, except to be thrown out and trampled underfoot by men. You are the light of the world. A city set on a hill cannot be hidden; nor does anyone light a lamp and put it under a basket, but on the lampstand, and it gives light to all who are in the house. Let your light shine before men in such a way that they may see your good works and glorify your Father who is in heaven."

—Matthew 5:13-16 (NASB)

35. Leaders Find Potential Key Leaders And Pour Their Lives Into Them.

Are you leaving a legacy? Live life in a way that reproduces what God has entrusted you with. What have you learned? What has He taught you? Find those who are willing to be taught and who are hungry for growth and pour your life experience into them. Leave a legacy by raising up others to follow after godly principles and values.

Father, let my life be spent giving out the truth of who You are. As You draw individuals to me, I will be faithful to lead them to You by sharing the truth from Your Word. Let my life influence many to follow after You, Lord.

"One generation shall praise Your works to another And shall declare Your mighty acts."

—*Psalm 145:4 (NASB)*

"And the things that you have heard from me among many witnesses, commit these to faithful men who will be able to teach others also."

—*2 Timothy 2:2 (NKJV)*

36. Set Captives Free And Ignite Them With God's Love.

By the Spirit of the Lord, you will help set people free as you walk in your God-given authority and anointing.

The freedom you have gained is the freedom you can release to others. You can only give what you have received. So, give what you have received. Freely you have received, freely give.

Father, by Your power and love, use me in the lives of others to break off the shackles that bind them. Empower them to live boldly for Christ as they make leading part of their everyday lifestyle.

"The Spirit of the LORD is upon Me, Because He has anointed Me To preach the gospel to the poor; He has sent Me to heal the brokenhearted, To proclaim liberty to the captives And recovery of sight to the blind, To set at liberty those who are oppressed."

—*Luke 4:18 (NKJV)*

"It shall come to pass in that day That his burden will be taken away from your shoulder, And his yoke from your neck, And the yoke will be destroyed because of the anointing oil."

—*Isaiah 10:27 (NKJV)*

37. If God Has Entrusted You With A Leadership Position, Don't Disqualify What He Has Qualified.

Stop criticizing yourself. Stop disqualifying what God has chosen. Stop allowing fear to control you.

Repent of it. God does not make mistakes. The Lord knows who He has chosen for such a time as this.

When we allow other people's rejection of us to stifle us or shut us down, we allow their insecurities to control and stop the will of God in us! Remember, the Lord promotes, and He brings down. If He has promoted you, then there is a reason for it. So, don't shrink back in fear. Trust in His ability to keep you.

He chose a young servant girl because her heart was ready to be used by God. She gave Him all the glory.

He chose Moses because of his humility, even though he lacked confidence.

If God has chosen you, then your feelings of inadequacy must be silenced.

Father, I choose to stand in whatever position and calling You see fit to give me. I will trust in Your ability to keep me and not in my inability to stand. I will not let my insecurities become excuses but a place of dependency on You.

"I am the Lord's servant," Mary answered. "May your word to me be fulfilled." Then the angel left her.

—*Luke 1:38 (NIV)*

"Then Moses said to the LORD, 'O my Lord, I am not eloquent, neither before nor since You have spoken to Your servant; but I am slow of speech and slow of tongue.'"

—Exodus 4:10 (NKJV)

38. A Good Leader Is A Good Delegator, One Who Leads By Example, By Telling You And By Showing You.

Joseph had been taken down to Egypt, but the Lord was with him, and he eventually became successful. Genesis 39:2 He did not allow hardship to define his future. He allowed his circumstances to grow him as an individual, and eventually he was noticed by Pharaoh, who called him into his God-determined position.

You may feel "taken out," but if God is for you, who can be against you? Good leaders allow life to mold them into strong, faithful leaders who can stand in the face of adversity and not shrink back. When you have been divinely shaped by life's circumstances, prepare yourself, for the doors of opportunity will open. So, be ready to walk through them. The time of preparation is now. Learn, teach others, and delegate.

Father, make me a great leader who can teach and delegate all that You have taught me.

Foster in me strong godly character that will stand the test of time. Use me for your glory.

"And Pharaoh said to Joseph, 'See, I have set you over all the land of Egypt.'"

—Genesis 41:41 (NKJV)

"He made him lord of his house And ruler over all his possessions."

—Psalm 105:21 (NKJV)

39. A Godly Leader Makes Hard Decisions For The Good Of All, Even When It's Costly.

The Word of God instructs us to allow God to teach us in the right path, for His eye is on us. God will choose to use those who are willing even when they have to pay a price. Are you willing to allow Christ to form His character in you so all that you do brings Him glory? Godly leadership requires soul-surrendered individuals who can trust the Lord, regardless of what God takes away and regardless of the difficulties.

Be strong in the Lord, for He will lead you in all truth, and your life will leave a legacy for others to follow.

Father, my soul is surrendered and submitted to you. I am willing for You to make me the godly leader You created me to be. I will trust You in every circumstance and allow the hard times of life to make me stronger, solidified in my resolve to live for You.

"I will instruct you and teach you in the way you should go; I will counsel you with my eye upon you."

—Psalm 32:8 (NASB)

"Have I not commanded you? Be strong and courageous. Do not be frightened, and do not be dismayed, for the LORD your God is with you wherever you go."

—Joshua 1:9 (ESV)

40. A Godly Leader Trusts God Completely! Their Lives Exemplify His Peace.

Regardless of what happens in life, God is in charge. If you belong to Him, He has you! As you bring all things to Him, His peace will be your portion. When you consistently walk in God's peace, you will consistently make godly decisions and grow in your ability to lead, even when things are difficult.

Father, I trust you completely and wholeheartedly. I desire to live in Your perfect peace. Your Word says perfect peace is mine as I keep my mind stayed on You. I choose to do so and I will grow as Your ambassador. I decree I am a kingdom-minded warrior growing in my leadership ability, and I will walk in the fullness of what You have called me to walk in.

"There are many plans in a man's heart, Nevertheless the Lord's counsel—that will stand."

—*Proverbs 19:21 (NKJV)*

"You will keep him in perfect peace, whose mind is stayed on You, because he trusts in You."

—*Isaiah 26:3 (NKJV)*

41. A Good Leader Recognizes Time-Stealers As Gum On A Shoe. Quickly Change Shoes.

We are all given the same amount of time each day. What are you doing with your time? Some people are sent by the enemy to steal your time and be a distraction in your life. Learn to discern who is sent from God and who is a demonic assignment meant to take you off course.

Father, teach us to number our days that we may gain a heart of wisdom. Teach us to redeem the time and give us discernment regarding those we are to invest time in and those who are distractions sent by the enemy.

"So teach us to number our days, That we may gain a heart of wisdom."

—Psalm 90:12 (NKJV)

"Walk in wisdom toward those who are outside, redeeming the time. Let your speech always be with grace, seasoned with salt, that you may know how you ought to answer each one."

—Colossians 4:5-6 (NKJV)

42. A Godly Leader Is Easily Recognized; Others Seek Out Your Counsel.

Do you want your life to add value to others? Do you want your life to matter and make an impact on others?

Become a leader who allows the Word of God to counsel and direct your steps. The Bible tells us in Psalm 1 that a blessed man prospers in every way because he or she delights and takes pleasure in living the Word of God. That person will prosper and be successful. When you walk in godly principles, you can help others do the same. Godly wisdom and Godly counsel will be a natural outflow when your life is governed by eternal principles.

Hear His Word and increase in learning. Be selective about who you let speak into your life. Choose character over charisma.

Father, teach me Your laws, and I will not sin against You. Your Word is my roadmap to a successful, God-enriched life, not only for me, but for those You have placed around me. I want to add value and increase their lives for good and not for evil. I choose to allow the Bible to be my source of wisdom and truth, and I will be selective about who I receive counsel from. Anoint me, Lord, to become one that others can trust to give good counsel.

"*A wise man will hear and increase in learning, And a man of understanding will attain wise counsel.*"

—*Proverbs 1:5 (NKJV)*

"Give instruction to a wise man, and he will be still wiser; Teach a just man and he will increase in learning."

—Proverbs 9:9 (NKJV)

43. A Good Leader Sees The Potential In Others And Is Willing To Invest The Time To Develop Them.

Jesus was the best example of godly leadership. The Bible states in John 15:13 that Jesus laid His life down for His friends.

Who are you investing in? Becoming a person of influence requires a selfless life. It requires spending time, talent, and treasure in those God has directed you to. See the potential in others and then give of your life. Speak from what you know and teach from what you have learned. As Jesus poured out His life to the disciples and taught them what He knew, we are also supposed to invest in the lives of those God has placed in our lives. Ask the Lord to give you His eyes to know who He has given you as your assignment, and be willing to pour your life into those people. When it is time to move from one person to another, be willing to move forward. Don't remain when God is moving you on.

Father, as You have developed in me Your heart to lead others, I will take what You have taught me and give it away. Show me whom you have chosen for me to invest in. As I give away what You have shown me, Father, continue to grow me and continue to mold me to be Your servant who always gives You glory.

"...we were well pleased to impart to you not only the gospel of God, but also our own lives, because you had become dear to us."

—1 Thessalonians 2:8 (NKJV)

"By this we know love, because He laid down His life for us. And we also ought to lay down our lives for the brethren."

—*1 John 3:16 (NKJV)*

44. Always Find One Thing You Learned From Your Challenge. Live And Grow Daily.

Challenges, trials, and hardships come to everyone. They are opportunities for you to grow. Growth comes when you can focus on what you have learned and how you can become better because of it. Joseph was divinely placed in a position of power and influence to save an entire nation but not without first being challenged, persecuted, and struck down. Yet through those circumstances, God gave him a heart to love the very ones who caused his heart horrendous pain because of the lost years he would never get back.

While Joseph knew he could never regain the years gone by, he also grew to understand that God could enrich, restore, and give him a future that far outweighed anything he had lost. He learned to live as a godly leader who did not misuse his power or expose the perpetrators.

What can you learn from your trial? How can you relate to Joseph in the injustice you went through? Ask the Lord to show you what redemption looks like for you. It's time to really live, not just survive. Don't allow the enemy of your soul to steal one more moment of your life. Learn from your challenge, grow, and live again. Make a difference in other people's lives. They will grow from your victories if you allow it.

Father, I may be hard-pressed by many pressures, but Your Word says I will not be crushed by them. I may feel perplexed and puzzled about what has happened, but I will not be in despair. I may have been persecuted and struck down, but I will not be forsaken, nor shall I be destroyed. Father, would You show me what redemption looks like in my life? I will take my redeemed life and become better, not bitter. Let my life be an example to others in how to love well, even when I have lived through an injustice.

"We are hard-pressed on every side, yet not crushed; we are perplexed, but not in despair; persecuted, but not forsaken; struck down, but not destroyed."

—*2 Corinthians 4:8-9 (NKJV)*

45. Challenges Are Opportunities To Grow.

God knows you by name. Your calling will produce challenges that should be viewed as opportunities for further growth. Like David, you are not an afterthought to God. You are His masterpiece. He will bring you opportunities through the challenges you face. Those challenges are a setup to your prosperity, to your success. When you can see them as opportunities for growth and not the reason you are being held back or the reason you are being kept from doing what you believe you should be doing, that is when your today comes into alignment with your tomorrow and you move forward in God's perfect timing.

The Lord will work everything together for good for those who love God and to those who are called according to His purpose. Romans 8:28 Instead of partnering with the enemy and complaining or being upset at your current trials, count it all joy! Remember, this current testing is making you perfect and complete so you will lack nothing! Your challenges are God's divine setups for your future growth. God knows your name. He knows where you live. He knows what He has created you for. Trust Him to take you through the process.

Father, though man looks at the outward, You look at the heart. Create in me a clean heart and renew a steadfast spirit within me. Psalm 51:10 I choose to see what You are doing in the trial and give you praise through it all. I trust You to cause this challenge in my life to perfect and complete me so that I lack no good thing.

"My brethren, count it all joy when you fall into various trials, knowing that the testing of your faith produces patience. But let patience have its perfect work, that you may be perfect and complete, lacking nothing."

—James 1:2-4 (NKJV)

"And we know that all things work together for good to those who love God, to those who are the called according to His purpose."

—Romans 8:28 (NKJV)

"The young lions lack and suffer hunger; but those who seek the LORD shall not lack any good thing."

—Psalm 34:10 (NKJV)

46. Adversity Is An Opportunity, Not A Limitation.

"The Lord is with you; mighty warrior, 'Go in the strength you have.'" The Lord appeared to Gideon and spoke these words in Judges 6.

Gideon told the Lord, "If the Lord is with us, why has all this happened to us? Where are all His wonders that our ancestors told us about when they said, 'Did not the Lord bring us up out of Egypt?' But now the Lord has abandoned us and given us into the hand of Midian."

In verse 14 we read, "Go in the strength you have and save Israel out of Midian's hand. Am I not sending you?"

You may relate to Gideon, who felt his tribe was the weakest in Manasseh, and he felt the least in his father's house. But the Lord responded in verse 16, "Surely I will be with you and you shall defeat the Midianites as one man."

Go in the strength you have, mighty warrior! The adversity you are experiencing is an opportunity for increase, not a limitation on your life! The Lord is the great deliverer and He will deliver you. Call upon His name and watch Him take you out of the closed winepress and into the open fields and spacious places!

God has called you and marked you out for this day and this hour. Go in the strength you have and watch Him make you a mighty warrior who will influence others for His glory!

Father, I decree Your Word over my life and not my feelings. I decree I am Your mighty warrior, and I will go in the strength I have, knowing You give strength to the weary and increase power to the weak!

"Many are the afflictions of the righteous, But the LORD delivers him out of them all."

—Psalm 34:19 (NKJV)

"Call upon Me in the day of trouble; I will deliver you, and you shall glorify Me."

—Psalm 50:15 (NKJV)

47. Great Leaders Don't Despise Small Beginnings.

David defeated the Philistine with a sling and one small stone. 1 Samuel 17:50

Mary became the mother of Jesus with one "yes" in her spirit!

Elisha received a double portion by watching Elijah when he was taken up by chariots.

You went from death to life with one decision to receive Christ.

Jesus said if you give a cup of cold water to the little ones, you will not lose your reward. Matthew 10:42

Great things begin with one small decision, one small step. One small action can bring about a tremendous change. Do not despise the day of small beginnings, for the Lord is delighted to see you begin!

He will promote you and increase your influence in time. One plants, another waters, but God gives the increase.

Father, I don't despise the day of small beginnings, but I am grateful for it! Take my life and make something beautiful with it. I am yours. Stretch me, teach me, and use me in a way that will bring You glory.

"Do not despise these small beginnings...."

—*Zechariah 4:10 (NLT)*

"For exaltation comes neither from the east Nor from the west nor from the south. But God is the Judge: He puts down one, And exalts another."

—Psalm 75:6-7 (NKJV)

48. Great Leaders Are Faithful Where They Are Planted.

Just do it! Do what is at hand to do. Be faithful right where you are planted. You are on your way to more. But before you can get there, you must be faithful right where you are! Being faithful not only requires action but also the right heart response. Faithfulness is one of the fruits of the Spirit found in Galatians 5:22. God knows your thoughts. Psalm 139:2 He will bring more opportunities and stretch wide your tent pegs, but it will require the right heart posture. David was faithful in tending the sheep in the field. In due season, God raised him up to be Israel's second king.

Moses was faithful to hear and obey the voice of God at the burning bush. So, God used him to deliver Israel from Egypt.

As you are faithful with little, God will add to it and make it much.

Father, increase my ability to steward Your way more and more. Teach me to be a godly leader, one that pours into others and causes no harm.

"Whoever is faithful with very little will also be faithful with much, and whoever is dishonest with very little will also be dishonest with much."

—Luke 16:10 (BSB)

"His lord said to him, 'Well done, good and faithful servant; you were faithful over a few things, I will make you ruler over many things. Enter into the joy of your lord."

—Matthew 25:21 (NKJV)

49. Great Leaders Exercise And Expand Their Gifts.

You have gifts from the Lord. Those gifts are not only for you, but also for others to enjoy and benefit from.

Don't dishonor God by devaluing or talking negatively about the gifts He has given you. Be thankful because the gifts are from Him. If you minimize your gifts or compare yourself to others and become discontent with the gifts you have, you are saying what He has done is not enough. The Word of God says that every good and perfect gift comes from Him. Learn to delight yourself in Him and what He has given you. The more you operate in your gifting, the stronger you grow in it! It's time to stir up the gifts in you. Ask the Lord for opportunities to use your gifts and be a blessing to those around you.

Father, You have given me good gifts to walk in so I could be a blessing. I ask You to stir those gifts inside me and give me opportunities to use my gifts to be a blessing to others.

"Every good and perfect gift is from above and comes down from the Father of lights, with whom there is no variation or shadow of turning."

—James 1:17 (NKJV)

"Therefore, I remind you to stir up the gift of God which is in you through the laying on of my hands."

—2 Timothy 1:6 (NKJV)

"As good stewards of the manifold grace of God, each of you should use whatever gift he has received to serve one another."

—1 Peter 4:10 (BSB)

50. Great Leaders Overcome Adversity.

Overcomers arise! You are more than conquerors in Christ. It is time to see yourself as God sees you and realize He has put a warrior inside you. Step up to the plate and walk in the calling you have been assigned. Since Christ has overcome the enemy, you are an overcomer as well. Every situation, every trial, every adversity you face is only an opportunity for you to advance His kingdom! Arise and take your rightful place, kingdom-minded warrior. Make a decision today that you will not be overcome by evil, but you will overcome evil with good!

Father, I choose to walk in my kingdom assignment today. I have the blood of Jesus running through my veins, and I will conquer those giants in front of me and succeed! No weapon formed against me shall prosper, but I will arise and run my race to overcome adversity for the glory of God.

"I write to you, fathers, Because you have known Him who is from the beginning. I write to you, young men, Because you have overcome the wicked one. I write to you, little children, because you have known the Father."

—*1 John 2:13 (NKJV)*

"Do not be overcome by evil, but overcome evil with good."

—*Romans 12:21 (NKJV)*

"Yet in all these things we are more than conquerors through Him who loved us."

—Romans 8:37 (NKJV)

"I have said these things to you, that in me you may have peace. In the world you will have tribulation. But take heart; I have overcome the world."

—John 16:33 (ESV)

51. Great Leaders Always Remember Where They Came From And Remain Humble.

Regardless of how far you may go, regardless of how much you may achieve, remember to do it all for the glory of God. Never forget where you came from. Humility is knowing your strength comes from Christ and not from yourself. You can be a powerful, anointed man or woman of God, but if you forget where your true strength comes from, you may become yesterday's man or woman. Ask the Lord to create in you a clean heart and renew a steadfast spirit within you. Stay in Christ daily and seek Him for every occasion. You will remain in His love and soar in all He has called you to do.

Father, in You I live and move and have my being. In the fear of the Lord, there is strong confidence. I will center my life in the fear of the Lord, and I know You will keep me in the palm of Your hands. Riches and honor are a byproduct of walking in the reverential fear and adoration of You, Lord.

"By humility and the fear of the LORD Are riches and honor and life."

—*Proverbs 22:4 (NKJV)*

"For the LORD takes delight in his people; he crowns the humble with victory."

—*Psalm 149:4 (NIV)*

"And whoever exalts himself will be humbled, and he who humbles himself will be exalted."

—*Matthew 23:12 (NKJV)*

"But He gives more grace. Therefore He says: 'God resists the proud, But gives grace to the humble.'"

—*James 4:6 (NKJV)*

52. Good Leaders Know What To Stress and What To Overlook

Knowing what to stress and what to overlook is not difficult if you make listening a priority. Proverbs 18:13 says to answer before listening is folly and shame. When we take time to listen, we can discern what is really happening and we can properly address it. Learning to hear beyond the words spoken is keen insight. Be quick to listen and slow to speak. James 1:19

Father, teach me to listen intently and discern correctly. Fill my understanding with wisdom to know what to stress and what to overlook.

"He who answers a matter before he hears it, it is folly and shame to him."

—*Proverbs 18:13 (NKJV)*

"My dear brothers and sisters, take note of this: Everyone should be quick to listen, slow to speak and slow to become angry."

—*James 1:19 (NIV)*

Meet The Author

Apostle Dr. Cathy Coppola ushers in the glory of God through worship; preaching His Word by the power of the Holy Spirit; and releasing His miracles, signs, and wonders to the nations.

She is the Apostle, Pastor, and founder of "Cathy Coppola International Ministries," "House of Glory Church," "Mighty Wind Broadcasting Network TV," and "Fired-Up Conferences." Her TV broadcast can be seen online daily at Mighty Wind Broadcasting Network TV, The Holy Spirit Broadcasting Network TV, Roku, Fire TV, Apple TV, and Spotify. You can also find her at cathycoppola.org, YouTube Apostle Cathy Coppola, MWBN.tv, and on social media.

Before Cathy Coppola ever had a relationship with Jesus, she heard the voice of God say to her in 1989, "Move to California. I'm doing a new thing, starting a new generation." Genesis 12:1-2 She and her husband had been married for two years and had a six-month-old child. Within one month, they left their family, their place of upbringing, and their jobs; sold their home; and moved to Southern California.

It was in California, in 1989, that she accepted Jesus as her Lord and Savior. In 1991 she was baptized and filled with the power of the Holy Spirit. She was filled with joy, taken up into a vision, and felt His love for the first time. Something significant happened to her in the baptismal waters. She saw heaven open up, and the supernatural realm seemed as if it were more real than the natural realm.

At that point, the Lord began healing her of years of emotional pain. The Lord said to her, "Cathy, a broken and contrite heart I will not despise." Psalm 51:17

The Lord began healing and delivering her from spirits of death, suicide, an eating disorder, fear, shame, worthlessness, and timidity.

Her life is marked by holy visitations and encounters. She describes her life as, "Ruined for the ordinary, radical for Jesus, and loving every moment."

Her ministry began after a powerful encounter with the Lord in 2009.

In this life-changing encounter, the Lord that launched her into full-time ministry visited her and took her to the Third Heaven. She found herself in a heavenly garden, a beautiful garden with Jesus. He showed her a flashback of her life and how His hand kept her from taking her life because He had a plan to display her for His glory. Then she went into an intense time of prophetically giving birth to her ministry. He gave her this mandate: "You are an injustice breaker. Break the injustice off My people! You will teach, and you will preach, but you will be known for signs and wonders." Then He asked her, "Will you go for Me? Will you be My mouthpiece to the nations?"

She responded with, "Yes, Lord. I will go wherever You

call me. I am Your handmaiden. Let it be done unto me according to Your Word."

Shortly after the vision, she began her prayer ministry in obedience to the Lord, to stand in the gap and contend for families who were being attacked by the enemy.

Her weekly services are full of the demonstration of the power of the Holy Spirit as He floods the meetings with signs, wonders, healings, and deliverances. It is a ministry where the physically sick are healed, the emotionally hurting are restored, those bound by demonic spirits are set free, and families are reconciled to their Heavenly Father's original design.

This weekly prayer meeting continued for seven years, and in the eighth year she birthed her church, House Of Glory. The church is dedicated to His presence, His healings, His miracles, an Apostolic calling to the nations.

One year after planting her church, the Holy Spirit spoke to her to launch her own TV ministry. Mighty Wind Broadcasting Network TV was birthed and was established to preach the Word, release His glory, and heal the sick.

It is her passion to minister to people and get them filled with the Holy Spirit and set free by His captivating love.

She was ordained a Pastor and Prophetess in 2014 and an Apostle in 2018. She has also received an honorary doctorate from Apostle Dr. Andrew Bills.

She describes herself as "one ordinary life that said yes to Jesus and the call of God." Her radical obedience and consistent responsiveness to Jesus in spite of her fears was fueled by her love for Him, which consumed her fear of man.

She is a sold-out, laid-down lover of Jesus, compelled by His love into a radical oneship with Him.

With a strong healing, deliverance, and prophetic gifting, she ministers to the nations, preaching God's Word and releasing His kingdom authority and power. She has ministered abroad in South America and Africa.

She has authored and published two other books, *From Grief to Glory* and *Devil! Get Your Hands Off!*

Cathy lives in California, USA, along with her husband of 35 years, their four adult children, and two grandchildren.

FOR MORE INFORMATION
Write to us at:
Cathy Coppola International Ministries
P.O. Box 2923
Mission Viejo, CA 92691

Visit our website
www.cathycoppola.org

Email us at:
cathycoppola@gmail.com

Made in the USA
Columbia, SC
07 July 2023